Phonics Bingo Ladders

NEW YORK • TORONTO • LONDON • AUCKLAND • SYDNEY
MEXICO CITY • NEW DELHI • HONG KONG • BUENOS AIRES

Teaching *Resources*

Written and conceived by Violet Findley
Book design by Brian LaRossa

ISBN-13: 978-0-545-22060-6 / ISBN-10: 0-545-22060-2
Copyright © 2010 by Scholastic Inc.

4 5 6 7 8 9 10   40   17 16 15 14 13 12

Contents

Introduction

Welcome to *Phonics Bingo Ladders*! Your students will learn how to play this engaging game is an instant, but the benefit of their playing it will last a lifetime.

That's because these engaging bingo ladders help children master 25 must-know phonics elements including *short vowels*, *long vowels*, *silent* e, *bossy* r, *blends*, and *digraphs*.

Research shows that repeated exposure to these elements helps lay the foundation for long-term reading success. Why? Systematic practice with key phonemes and letter clusters provides children with a "mental toolbox" they can instantly access to decode the hundreds of words they encounter each day. And decoding agility leads to reading fluency—the ultimate goal for all young learners.

Research also shows that one of the best ways for children to internalize the rules of phonics is through meaningful skill-and-drill activities. That's where this great book comes in.

A few minutes a day or week is all it takes to integrate these bingo ladders into your weekly routine. Treat the whole class to a quick game just before the bell rings. Or place laminated sets in a learning center for small groups or pairs to play independently. Make bingo ladders a classroom habit—and watch your students' reading skills soar!

Skills Covered:

Short a, short e, short i, short o, short u, long a, long e, long i, long o, long u, silent e, bossy r, br, ch, cl; fl, gr, pr, sh, sl, sp, st, sw, th, and tr.

Standards Covered:

The bingo games in this book are designed to support you in meeting these essential K–2 standards:

✓ Uses the general skills and strategies of the reading process.

✓ Understands level-appropriate sight words and vocabulary.

✓ Uses phonemic analysis to decode unknown words.

✓ Uses structural analysis to decode unknown words.

Source: *Content Knowledge: A Compendium of Standards and Benchmarks for PreK–12 Education,* (4th edition). (Mid-Continent Regional Educational Laboratory, 2004)

Preparing the Games for Play

To make each of the 25 bingo games, follow these simple directions:

1. Choose the phonics element you want to teach, for example *long e*. Make a photocopy of the six bingo ladders, chart, and cards for that set of words. (Tip: For whole-class play, make duplicate copies of the ladders so that every child gets one.)

2. Cut the bingo ladders and word cards apart along the dashed lines.

3. Optional: Color the ladders to make them extra appealing. Laminate the bingo ladders, charts, and cards to make them extra strong.

4. Purchase or prepare markers for the game such as plastic discs, dried beans, buttons, or the reproducible markers on pages 88 and 89. Also prepare a brown bag or box with the phonics element (for example, *"long e"*) written on it.

5. Store each phonics game in a labeled manila envelope.

Components

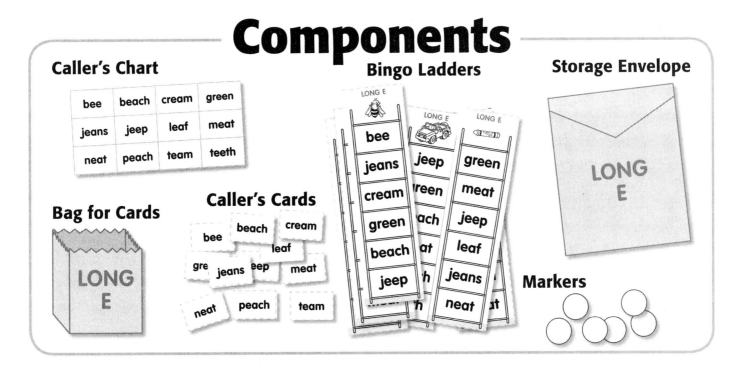

Caller's Chart

bee	beach	cream	green
jeans	jeep	leaf	meat
neat	peach	team	teeth

Bingo Ladders

LONG E
bee
jeans
cream
green
beach
jeep

LONG E
jeep
reen
ach
at
h

LONG E
green
meat
jeep
leaf
jeans
neat

Storage Envelope

LONG E

Bag for Cards

LONG E

Caller's Cards

beach   cream
bee
leaf
gre   jeans   eep   meat
neat   peach   team

Markers

How to Play

The games in this book can be played by the whole class, small groups, or pairs. Here are the easy instructions:

1. Choose the phonics element you want to focus on, such as *long e*. (Tip: You can also use the blank templates on pages 85–87 to teach a phonics elements not included in this book.)

2. Make multiple copies of the bingo ladders for that set and distribute one to each student.

3. Give each student six markers.

4. Invite a student volunteer to act as the caller (or do so yourself). Provide the caller with the Caller's Chart and a brown bag or box filled with the cut-apart word cards.

5. Ask the caller to pull out a card (such as *jeep*), read it aloud, and place it on the Caller's Chart.

6. When a word appears on a student's board, he/she covers it with a marker.

7. Play continues with the caller reading aloud each word and students covering the words with markers. When a student has covered all six words on his/her ladder, that student shouts, "Phonics Bingo!"

8. The caller should then check the answers to make sure that student is, in fact, a winner. If so, lead students in round of applause. (NOTE: If you are playing with multiples copies of the same bingo ladders, there will be multiple winners.)

Phonics Activities to Extend Learning

Reinforce phonemic awareness with a variety of quick listening activities, such as the following:

Listen Up!

✓ Tell children that you are going to say some words that contain the sound you are studying (*slug, slime, slump*). You will also say a word that doesn't belong (*flat*). When they hear the word that doesn't belong, they are to say "Buzzzz!" For a variation, gather children in an open area and invite them to run around you as you shout out words that have the same phonics element. When they hear the word that doesn't belong, they should "freeze."

✓ Make letter cards for *a, e, i, o,* and *u*. Distribute a set to each child. Tell children you are going to say a word that contains a short vowel, such as *pig*. Have children hold up the correct vowel (*i*). Continue in this manner with other short-vowel words. On another day, repeat the activity with words that contain long vowels.

✓ Choose a digraph such as *sh*. Tell children you are going to say some words, and they are to tell you if they hear the featured sound at the beginning or end of the word. If they hear the sound at the beginning (as in *ship*), they should put their fingers to their lips and say "shhh." If they hear the sound at the end (as in *dish*), they should put their hands together and wiggle them like a fish. Repeat the activity with other digraphs and movements.

✓ For multisyllabic words, tell children you are going to say some words and they are going to clap to show how many syllables, or word parts, they hear. For example, if you say the word *grasshopper*, they will clap three times: *grass* (clap)… *hop* (clap)… *er* (clap). Repeat the activity with other multisyllabic words.

Silly Sentences

Write a silly sentence on the board that contains several words featuring a target sound, such as *tr*. Include an underlined word that is one or two letters from being correct, for example: *The tricky trolls traveled on a choo-choo <u>grain</u>*. Ask a volunteer to change the letter(s) to form a word that makes sense in the sentence (*train*). Have children erase the old word and write the new one in its place. Continue with other silly sentences.

Phonics Toss

Arrange children into two or three teams. Divide a big sheet of drawing paper into five sections. Write a vowel, blend, or digraph in each section. Then challenge children to a beanbag toss. Have team members take turns tossing the beanbag onto the paper. When the beanbag lands, have the child say the phonics sound in that section and think of a word that begins with that sound. Write the words on the chalkboard, keeping separate columns for each team. Players earn one point for each word.

Phonics Pop-Up Game

Select a phonics sound, such as *short a*. Write words containing that sound on index cards. List the same words on a piece of paper (for you to read). Have children sit in a circle, and give each one a word card. Explain that when they hear their word, they are to pop up on their feet and hold up their card. After all the cards have been read, redistribute them to play again. Encourage children to see if they can improve their speed.

Reading 'Round the Room

Invite children to search around the room for items with a target sound, such as *long o*. Have children write the name of the object on a sticky note and place it on the object. You can also give children clues, such as "I spy something that is round. It represents the world." (globe) When you are finished working with that particular sound, collect the sticky notes and place them on index cards. Add these to your collection of word cards.

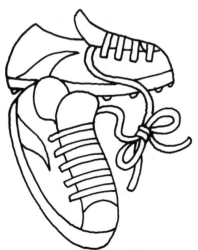

Terrific Tongue Twisters

Choose a target sound to work with, such as *sh*. Write a tongue twister on the board that features the sound, for example: *Shelly Sharp shopped for shiny shoes.* Say it once slowly and then challenge children to say it five times fast. When you are done, invite groups of children to invent their own phonics tongue twisters to share with the class.

Phonics Bingo Ladders

bike

cake

drum

CALLER'S CHART

cat	bad	fan	gas
jazz	map	pad	ram
sad	tack	van	yam

CALLER'S CARDS

cat	bad	fan	gas
jazz	map	pad	ram
sad	tack	van	yam

SHORT A

cat

bad

fan

gas

jazz

map

SHORT A

ram

sad

pad

tack

van

yam

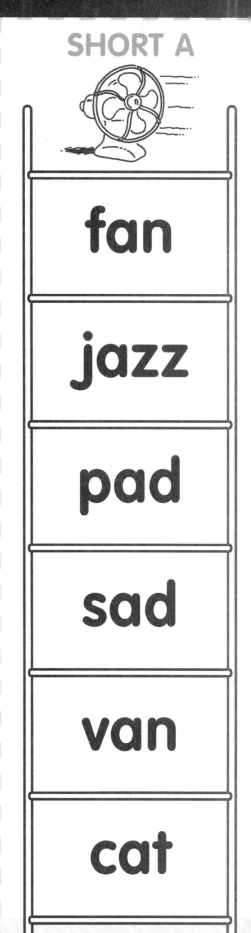

SHORT A

fan

jazz

pad

sad

van

cat

SHORT A

| map |
| tack |
| gas |
| bad |
| ram |
| yam |

SHORT A

| van |
| cat |
| yam |
| bad |
| fan |
| tack |

SHORT A

| sad |
| gas |
| map |
| pad |
| jazz |
| ram |

CALLER'S CHART

bed	bell	dress	help
jet	men	peck	red
send	ten	wet	yes

CALLER'S CARDS

bed	bell	dress	help
jet	men	peck	red
send	ten	wet	yes

SHORT E

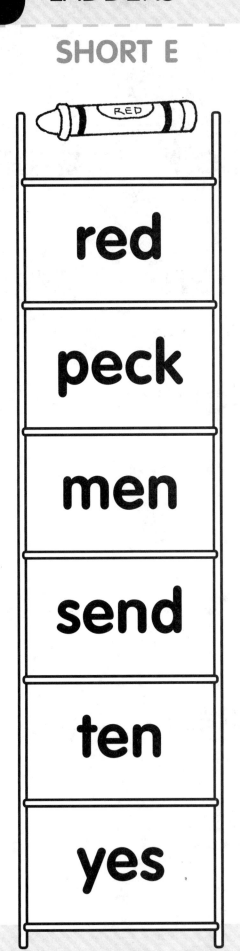

bed
bell
men
help
jet
dress

SHORT E

red
peck
men
send
ten
yes

SHORT E

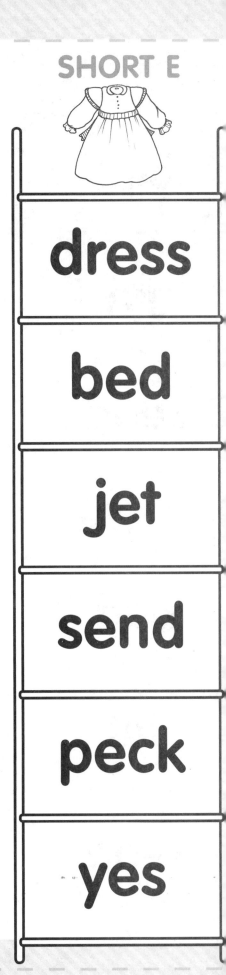

dress
bed
jet
send
peck
yes

SHORT E

bell
help
men
wet
ten
red

SHORT E

10

ten
bell
dress
bed
wet
yes

SHORT E

jet
help
wet
peck
red
send

CALLER'S CHART

bib	dip	fish	gift
hill	lid	milk	pig
rib	sit	sink	wig

CALLER'S CARDS

bib	dip	fish	gift
hill	lid	milk	pig
rib	sit	sink	wig

SHORT I

SHORT I

SHORT I

hill	milk	bib
dip	sit	hill
fish	rib	fish
gift	pig	milk
lid	sink	rib
bib	wig	sink

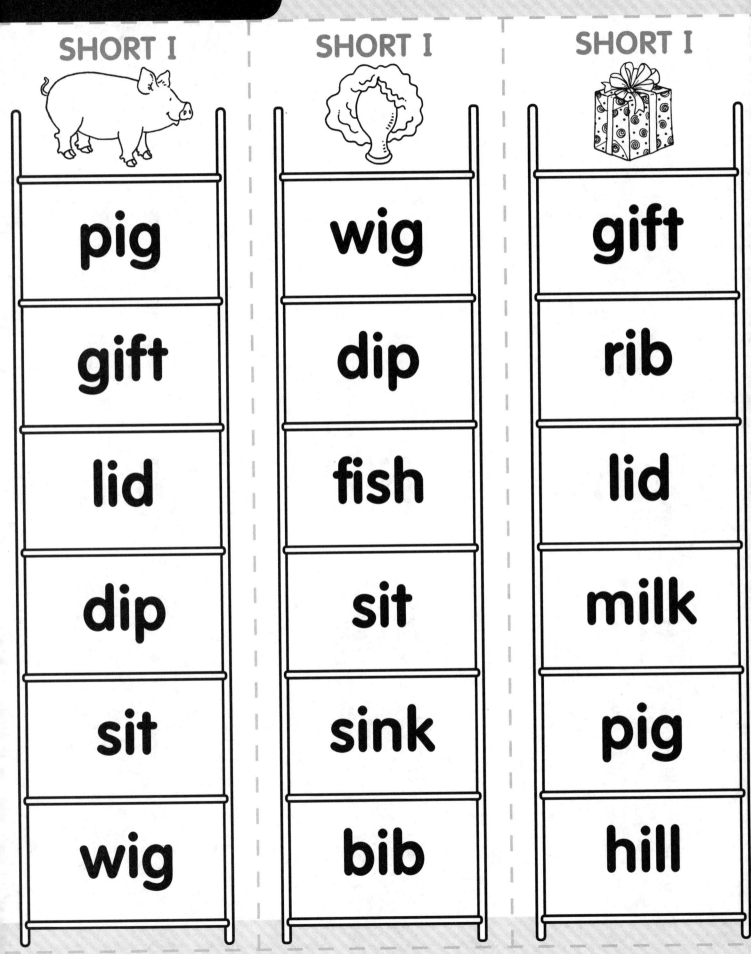

SHORT I

pig
gift
lid
dip
sit
wig

SHORT I

wig
dip
fish
sit
sink
bib

SHORT I

gift
rib
lid
milk
pig
hill

CALLER'S CHART

block	box	clock	cot
fox	jog	log	pot
rock	shop	sock	top

CALLER'S CARDS

block	box	clock	cot
fox	jog	log	pot
rock	shop	sock	top

SHORT O

box
block
clock
cot
fox
jog

SHORT O

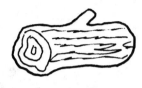

log
shop
rock
pot
sock
top

SHORT O

rock
clock
fox
log
block
sock

SHORT O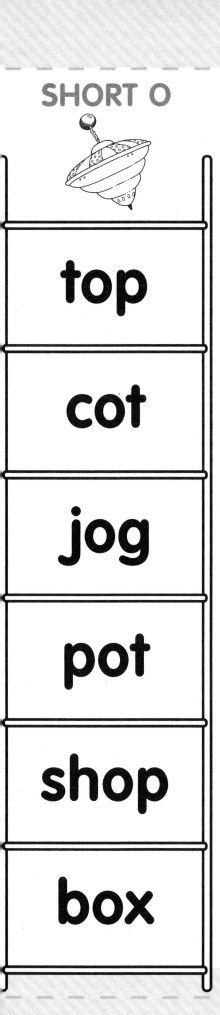

SHORT O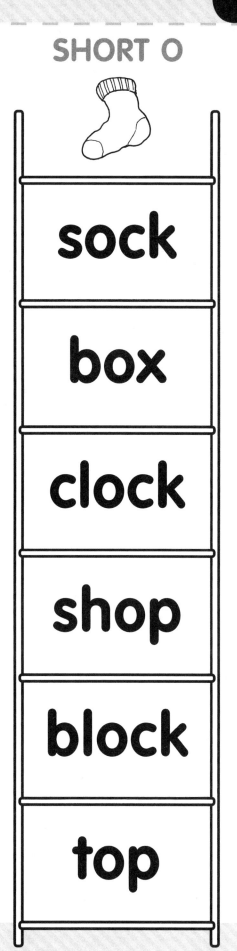

SHORT O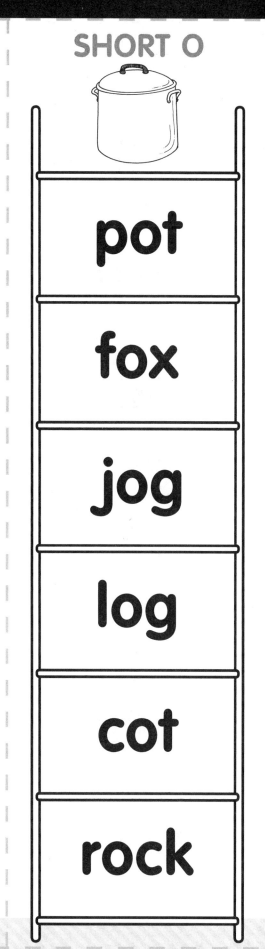

top	sock	pot
cot	box	fox
jog	clock	jog
pot	shop	log
shop	block	cot
box	top	rock

CALLER'S CHART

bug	duck	drum	fun
jump	mug	nut	pup
rug	sun	truck	tub

CALLER'S CARDS

bug	duck	drum	fun
jump	mug	nut	pup
rug	sun	truck	tub

SHORT U

bug
duck
drum
mug
jump
fun

SHORT U

tub
pup
rug
sun
truck
nut

SHORT U

truck
drum
jump
nut
rug
bug

SHORT U

SHORT U

SHORT U

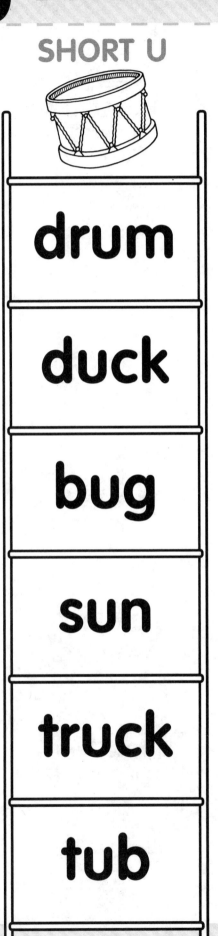

duck	drum	mug
pup	duck	jump
mug	bug	fun
fun	sun	nut
sun	truck	pup
tub	tub	rug

24

cake	chain	flame	grapes
lake	maze	plate	rain
rake	skate	tape	train

CALLER'S CARDS

cake	chain	flame	grapes
lake	maze	plate	rain
rake	skate	tape	train

LONG A

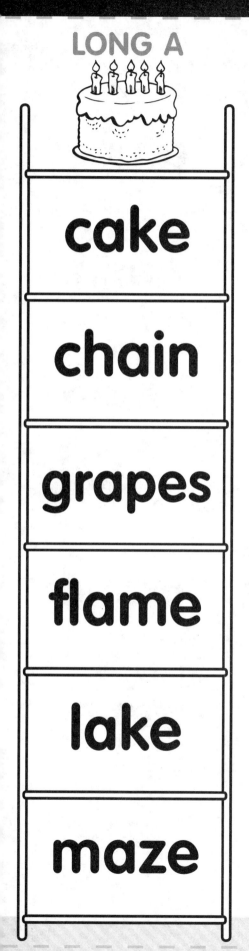

cake

chain

grapes

flame

lake

maze

LONG A

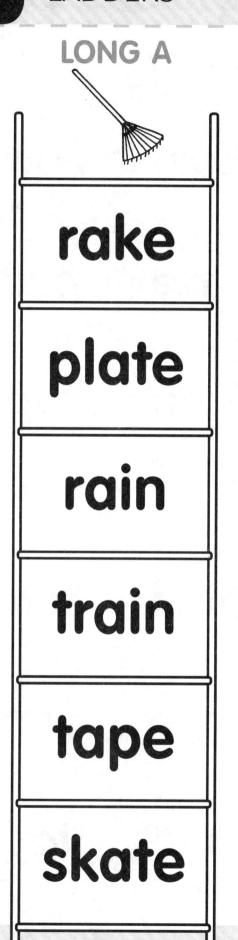

rake

plate

rain

train

tape

skate

LONG A

tape

flame

lake

plate

rake

cake

LONG A

| grapes |
| chain |
| skate |
| rain |
| maze |
| train |

LONG A

| skate |
| chain |
| flame |
| cake |
| tape |
| train |

LONG A

| maze |
| rake |
| grapes |
| plate |
| rain |
| lake |

CALLER'S CHART

bee	beach	cream	green
jeans	jeep	leaf	meat
neat	peach	team	teeth

CALLER'S CARDS

bee	beach	cream	green
jeans	jeep	leaf	meat
neat	peach	team	teeth

LONG E

| bee |
| jeans |
| cream |
| green |
| beach |
| jeep |

LONG E

| leaf |
| teeth |
| neat |
| peach |
| team |
| meat |

LONG E

| jeans |
| cream |
| bee |
| team |
| neat |
| leaf |

LONG E

jeep
green
beach
meat
peach
teeth

LONG E

teeth
beach
cream
peach
team
bee

LONG E

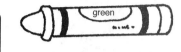

green
meat
jeep
leaf
jeans
neat

CALLER'S CHART

bike	five	hive	ice
kite	lime	mice	pine
rise	side	shine	white

CALLER'S CARDS

bike	five	hive	ice
kite	lime	mice	pine
rise	side	shine	white

LONG I

bike
lime
hive
ice
kite
five

LONG I

mice
shine
rise
side
pine
white

LONG I

kite
hive
bike
mice
rise
shine

LONG I

| five |
| ice |
| lime |
| side |
| pine |
| white |

LONG I

| hive |
| five |
| bike |
| side |
| shine |
| white |

LONG I
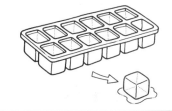

| ice |
| rise |
| lime |
| mice |
| pine |
| kite |

CALLER'S CHART

boat	bone	coach	code
goat	globe	hose	phone
road	smoke	soap	toad

CALLER'S CARDS

boat	bone	coach	code
goat	globe	hose	phone
road	smoke	soap	toad

LONG O

boat
globe
coach
code
goat
bone

LONG O

hose
smoke
road
phone
soap
toad

LONG O

goat
coach
boat
hose
road
soap

35

LONG O

| globe |
| code |
| bone |
| phone |
| smoke |
| toad |

LONG O

| soap |
| bone |
| coach |
| smoke |
| boat |
| toad |

LONG O

| phone |
| goat |
| globe |
| hose |
| code |
| road |

CALLER'S CHART

bugle	cube	cute	fume
future	huge	human	menu
mule	music	tube	use

CALLER'S CARDS

bugle	cube	cute	fume
future	huge	human	menu
mule	music	tube	use

LONG U

- bugle
- huge
- cute
- fume
- future
- cube

LONG U

- mule
- use
- human
- music
- tube
- menu

LONG U

- tube
- cute
- future
- human
- mule
- bugle

LONG U

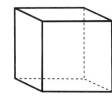

- cube
- use
- huge
- menu
- music
- fume

LONG U

- music
- cube
- cute
- bugle
- tube
- use

LONG U

- human
- future
- huge
- fume
- menu
- mule

CALLER'S CHART

bride	gate	hide	hole
kite	late	mule	nose
robe	snake	tube	wave

CALLER'S CARDS

bride	gate	hide	hole
kite	late	mule	nose
robe	snake	tube	wave

SILENT E

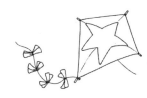

- kite
- bride
- late
- gate
- hide
- tube

SILENT E

- snake
- nose
- robe
- mule
- tube
- wave

SILENT E

- gate
- kite
- late
- hole
- mule
- wave

SILENT E

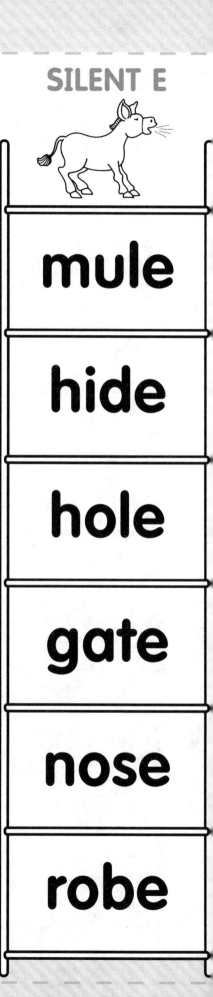

SILENT E	SILENT E	SILENT E
nose	bride	mule
hide	tube	hide
hole	kite	hole
bride	snake	gate
snake	late	nose
wave	robe	robe

CALLER'S CHART

bird	car	clerk	dark
girl	fort	her	horse
nurse	purse	star	turn

CALLER'S CARDS

bird	car	clerk	dark
girl	fort	her	horse
nurse	purse	star	turn

LADDERS

BOSSY R

bird
fort
clerk
dark
girl
car

BOSSY R

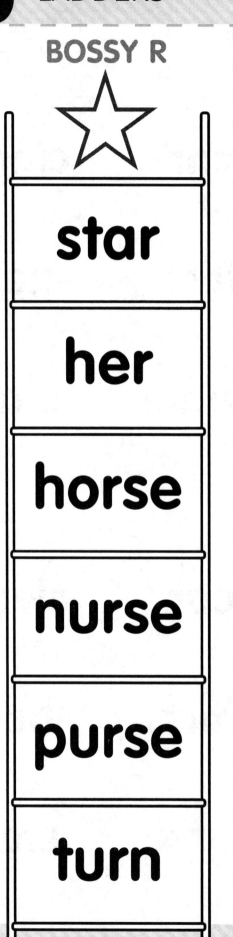

star
her
horse
nurse
purse
turn

BOSSY R

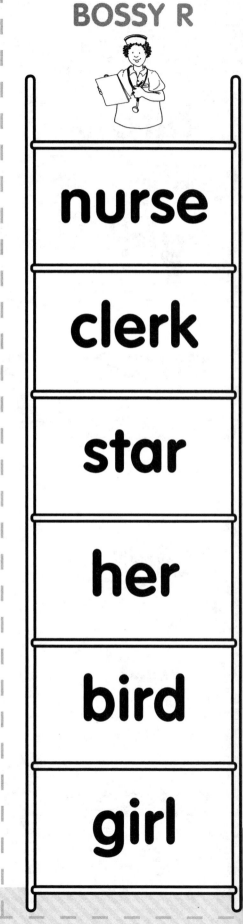

nurse
clerk
star
her
bird
girl

BOSSY R

car

fort

dark

horse

purse

turn

BOSSY R

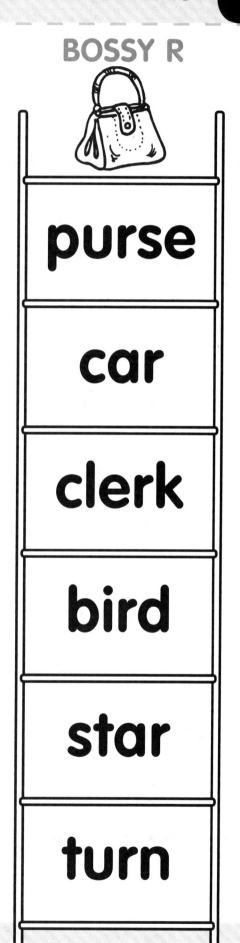

purse

car

clerk

bird

star

turn

BOSSY R

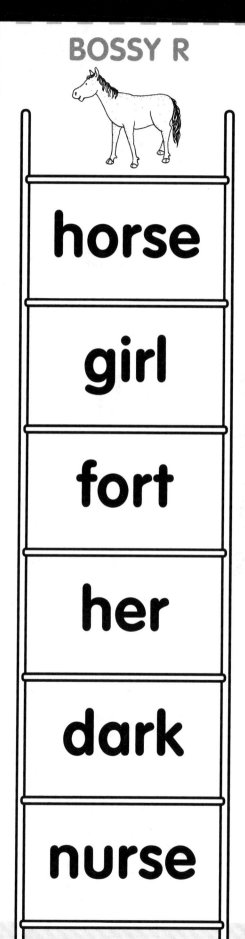

horse

girl

fort

her

dark

nurse

CALLER'S CHART

braid	brain	brake	branch
bread	breeze	brick	bridge
bright	broom	brown	brush

CALLER'S CARDS

braid	brain	brake	branch
bread	breeze	brick	bridge
bright	broom	brown	brush

BR BLENDS

BR BLENDS

- braid
- brake
- brain
- branch
- bread
- breeze

BR BLENDS

- brush
- brick
- bridge
- bright
- broom
- breeze

BR BLENDS

- bread
- brake
- braid
- brick
- bright
- brown

BR BLENDS

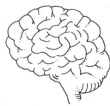

- brain
- branch
- bridge
- breeze
- broom
- brush

BR BLENDS

- broom
- brain
- brake
- braid
- brown
- brush

BR BLENDS

- branch
- brick
- brown
- bread
- bridge
- bright

CALLER'S CHART

chair	chalk	cheap	checkers
cheese	cherry	chew	chick
child	chin	chip	chop

CALLER'S CARDS

chair	chalk	cheap	checkers
cheese	cherry	chew	chick
child	chin	chip	chop

CH DIGRAPHS

chair

chalk

cherry

checkers

cheese

cheap

CH DIGRAPHS

chick

chew

child

chin

chip

chop

CH DIGRAPHS

cheese

cheap

chair

chew

child

chip

CH DIGRAPHS

CH DIGRAPHS

chalk

checkers

chin

chick

cherry

chop

CH DIGRAPHS

chin

chalk

cheap

chair

chip

chop

CH DIGRAPHS

cherry

cheese

checkers

chew

chick

child

CALLER'S CHART

clam	clang	class	clay
cliff	climate	clock	clothes
clown	cloud	clue	cluck

CALLER'S CARDS

clam	clang	class	clay
cliff	climate	clock	clothes
clown	cloud	clue	cluck

CL BLENDS

CL BLENDS

clam

class

clang

clay

cliff

climate

CL BLENDS

clock

cluck

clown

cloud

clue

clothes

CL BLENDS

clown

class

cliff

clock

clam

clue

CL BLENDS

CL BLENDS

- cloud
- clay
- climate
- clothes
- clang
- cluck

CL BLENDS

- clothes
- clam
- class
- cloud
- clue
- cluck

CL BLENDS

- clay
- clown
- climate
- clock
- clang
- cliff

CALLER'S CHART

flag	flake	flame	flap
flea	float	flock	flood
floor	flower	flute	fly

CALLER'S CARDS

flag	flake	flame	flap
flea	float	flock	flood
floor	flower	flute	fly

FL BLENDS

flag
float
flame
flap
flea
flake

FL BLENDS

fly
flood
floor
flower
flute
flock

FL BLENDS

flute
flake
flea
flock
floor
flag

FL BLENDS

FL BLENDS

| flower |
| flame |
| flap |
| float |
| flood |
| fly |

FL BLENDS

| flame |
| flake |
| flag |
| flower |
| flute |
| fly |

FL BLENDS

| flock |
| flap |
| float |
| flea |
| flood |
| floor |

GR BLENDS

CALLER'S CHART

grab	grain	grandpa	grapes
grass	grasshopper	green	grew
grind	ground	growl	gruff

CALLER'S CARDS

grab	grain	grandpa	grapes
grass	grasshopper	green	grew
grind	ground	growl	gruff

GR BLENDS

GR BLENDS

- grapes
- grass
- grandpa
- grab
- grain
- grasshopper

GR BLENDS

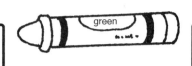

- green
- ground
- grind
- grew
- grass
- gruff

GR BLENDS

- growl
- grass
- grandpa
- green
- grind
- grab

GR BLENDS

grasshopper

green

grain

grapes

ground

gruff

GR BLENDS

grandpa

grain

grab

ground

growl

gruff

GR BLENDS

grass

grind

grasshopper

growl

grew

grapes

CALLER'S CHART

practice	present	pretty	pretzel
price	prince	princess	print
prize	problem	proud	prune

CALLER'S CARDS

practice	present	pretty	pretzel
price	prince	princess	print
prize	problem	proud	prune

PR BLENDS

present

practice

pretty

proud

price

princess

PR BLENDS

prince

prune

print

prize

problem

princess

PR BLENDS

pretzel

pretty

practice

prize

print

prune

PR BLENDS

| price |
| pretzel |
| prince |
| print |
| problem |
| present |

PR BLENDS

| princess |
| present |
| pretty |
| problem |
| proud |
| prune |

PR BLENDS

| prize |
| price |
| prince |
| practice |
| proud |
| pretzel |

SH DIGRAPHS

CALLER'S CHART

shack	shade	shadow	shampoo
shark	shave	shell	shelf
shoe	shine	shoulder	shower

CALLER'S CARDS

shack	shade	shadow	shampoo
shark	shave	shell	shelf
shoe	shine	shoulder	shower

SH DIGRAPHS

SH DIGRAPHS

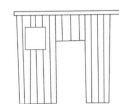

shack

shave

shadow

shampoo

shark

shade

SH DIGRAPHS

shell

shine

shoe

shelf

shoulder

shower

SH DIGRAPHS

shark

shadow

shack

shell

shoe

shoulder

SH DIGRAPHS

shampoo

shade

shave

shelf

shine

shell

SH DIGRAPHS

shower

shade

shadow

shine

shoulder

shack

SH DIGRAPHS

shoe

shark

shave

shower

shelf

shampoo

CALLER'S CHART

slab	slant	sled	sleep
sleeve	slice	slide	slipper
slope	slug	slow	sly

CALLER'S CARDS

slab	slant	sled	sleep
sleeve	slice	slide	slipper
slope	slug	slow	sly

SL BLENDS

sled

slant

slab

sleep

sleeve

slice

SL BLENDS

slide

slipper

slug

slope

slow

sly

SL BLENDS

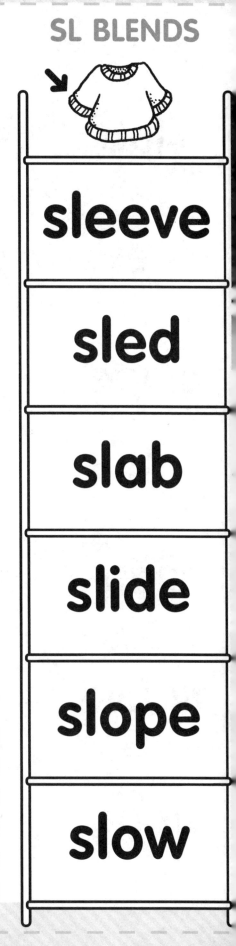

sleeve

sled

slab

slide

slope

slow

SL BLENDS

| slipper |
| sleep |
| slice |
| slant |
| slug |
| sly |

SL BLENDS

| slug |
| slant |
| sled |
| slab |
| slope |
| sly |

SL BLENDS

| sleep |
| sleeve |
| slice |
| slide |
| slipper |
| slow |

CALLER'S CHART

space	spark	speak	spear
speed	spike	spill	spine
spoil	sponge	sprout	spy

CALLER'S CARDS

space	spark	speak	spear
speed	spike	spill	spine
spoil	sponge	sprout	spy

SP BLENDS

- space
- spark
- speak
- spear
- speed
- spill

SP BLENDS

- spill
- spine
- spoil
- sponge
- sprout
- spy

SP BLENDS

- spine
- speak
- speed
- spike
- sprout
- space

SP BLENDS

sponge
spear
spike
spoil
spark
spy

SP BLENDS

speak
spark
spy
sponge
sprout
space

SP BLENDS

spear
speed
spike
spill
spine
spoil

CALLER'S CHART

stack	stairs	stamp	stapler
star	sticky	stomach	stone
stool	store	storm	story

CALLER'S CARDS

stack	stairs	stamp	stapler
star	sticky	stomach	stone
stool	store	storm	story

ST BLENDS

star

stairs

stamp

stapler

stack

sticky

ST BLENDS

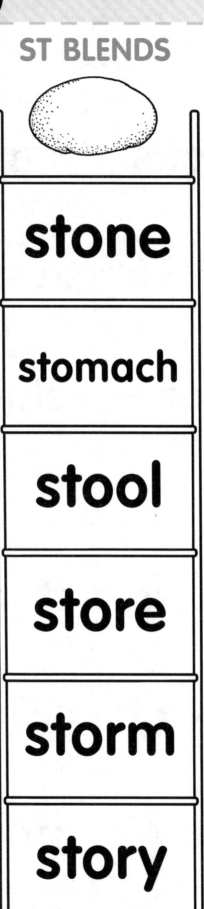

stone

stomach

stool

store

storm

story

ST BLENDS

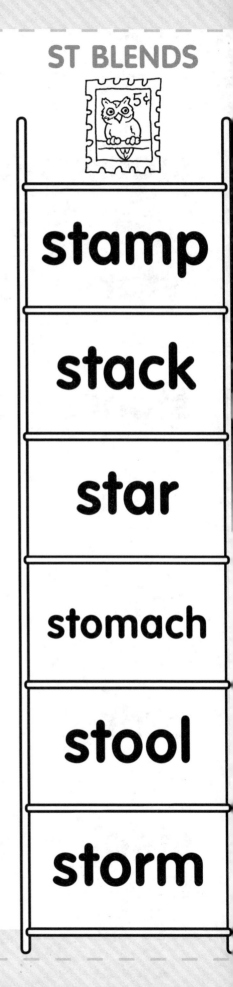

stamp

stack

star

stomach

stool

storm

ST BLENDS

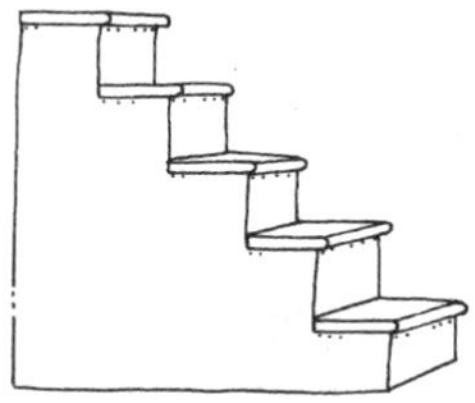

stairs

stapler

story

stone

store

sticky

ST BLENDS

storm

stairs

stamp

store

stack

story

ST BLENDS

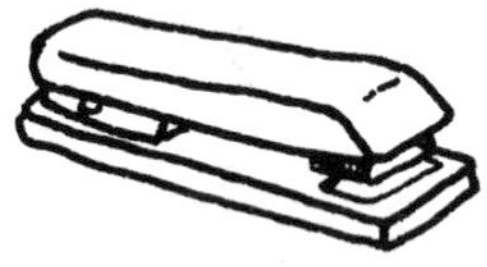

stapler

star

sticky

stomach

stone

story

CALLER'S CHART

swallow	swarm	swamp	swan
sway	sweater	sweep	sweet
swift	swim	swollen	swoop

CALLER'S CARDS

swallow	swarm	swamp	swan
sway	sweater	sweep	sweet
swift	swim	swollen	swoop

SW BLENDS

sweater

swarm

swamp

swan

sway

swallow

SW BLENDS

sweep

sweet

swim

swift

swollen

swoop

SW BLENDS

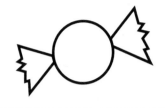

sweet

swallow

sway

sweep

swift

swollen

SW BLENDS

| swarm |
| swan |
| sweater |
| sweet |
| swim |
| swoop |

SW BLENDS

| swim |
| swarm |
| swamp |
| swallow |
| swollen |
| swoop |

SW BLENDS

| swan |
| sway |
| sweater |
| sweep |
| swamp |
| swift |

CALLER'S CHART

thank	thaw	thick	thief
thimble	thin	think	thirteen
thirst	thorn	thumb	thunder

CALLER'S CARDS

thank	thaw	thick	thief
thimble	thin	think	thirteen
thirst	thorn	thumb	thunder

TH DIGRAPHS

- thimble
- thaw
- thick
- thief
- thank
- thin

TH DIGRAPHS

- think
- thirteen
- thorn
- thirst
- thumb
- thunder

TH DIGRAPHS

- thumb
- thick
- thimble
- thin
- think
- thank

TH DIGRAPHS

thirteen

thief

thin

thaw

thorn

thunder

TH DIGRAPHS

thorn

thaw

thick

thank

thumb

thunder

TH DIGRAPHS

thunder

thimble

think

thin

thirteen

thirst

TR BLENDS

CALLER'S CHART

trace	track	train	trash
tray	tree	troll	trot
trouble	trumpet	trunk	try

CALLER'S CARDS

trace	track	train	trash
tray	tree	troll	trot
trouble	trumpet	trunk	try

TR BLENDS

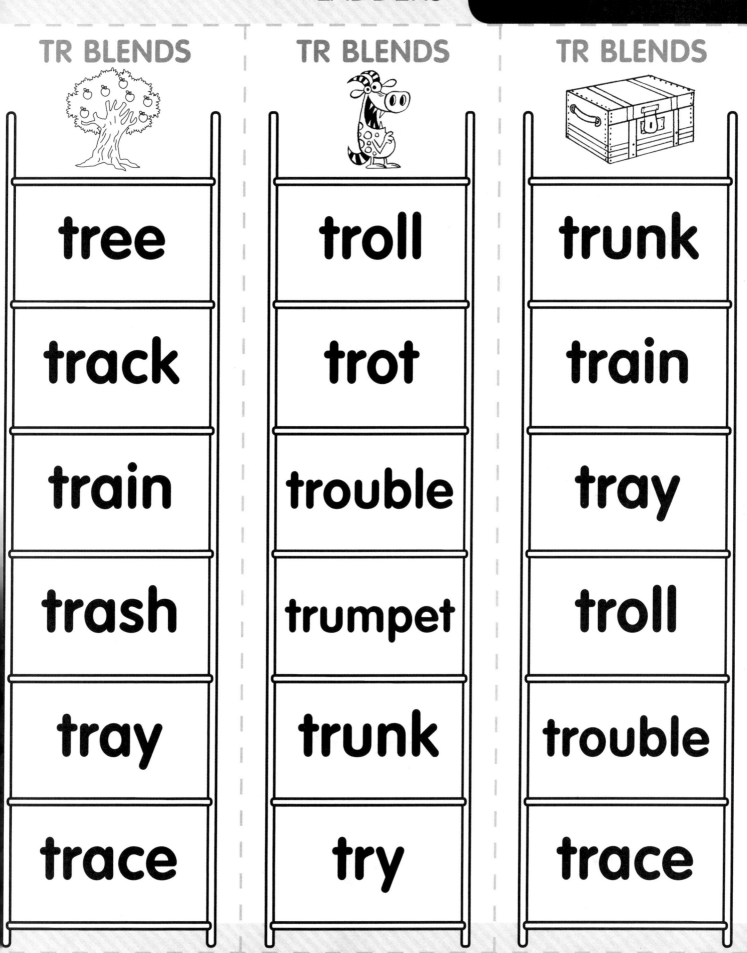

tree

track

train

trash

tray

trace

TR BLENDS

troll

trot

trouble

trumpet

trunk

try

TR BLENDS

trunk

train

tray

troll

trouble

trace

TR BLENDS

track

tree

trash

trot

trumpet

try

TR BLENDS

trumpet

track

train

trace

trunk

try

TR BLENDS

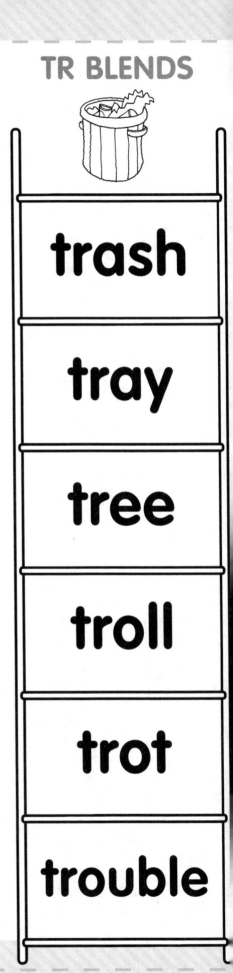

trash

tray

tree

troll

trot

trouble

CALLER'S CHART

CALLER'S CARDS

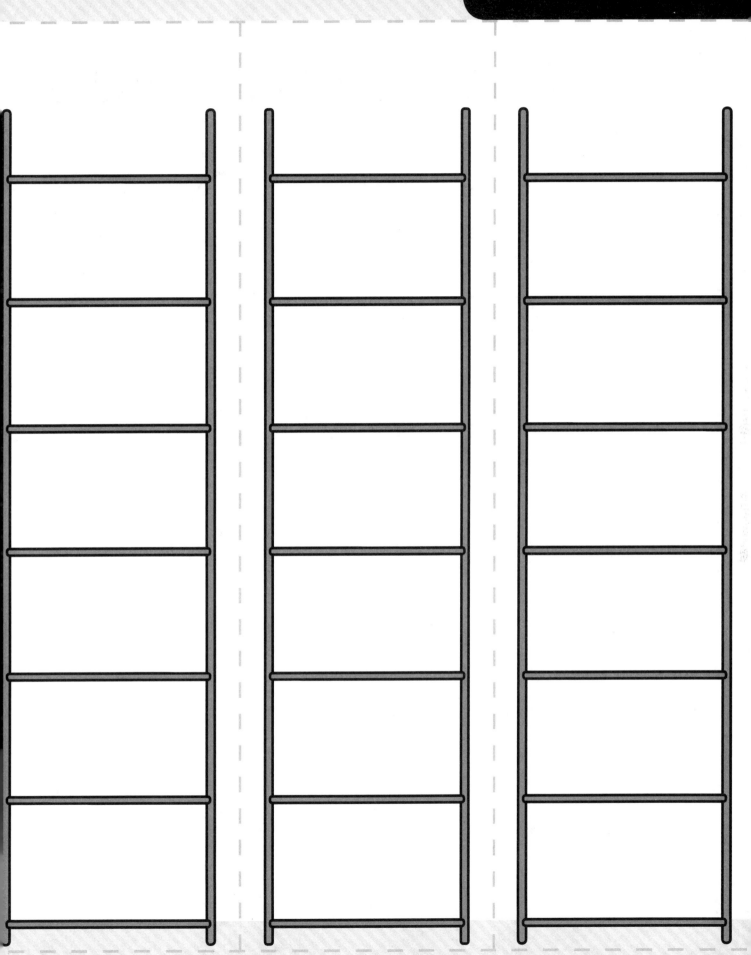

Reproducible Markers (Circles)

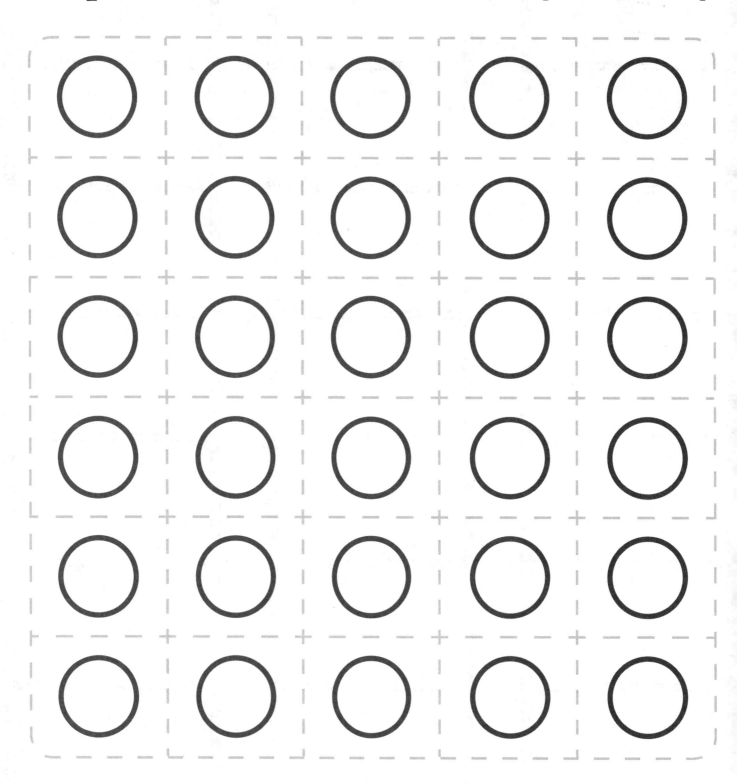

Reproducible Markers (Stars)

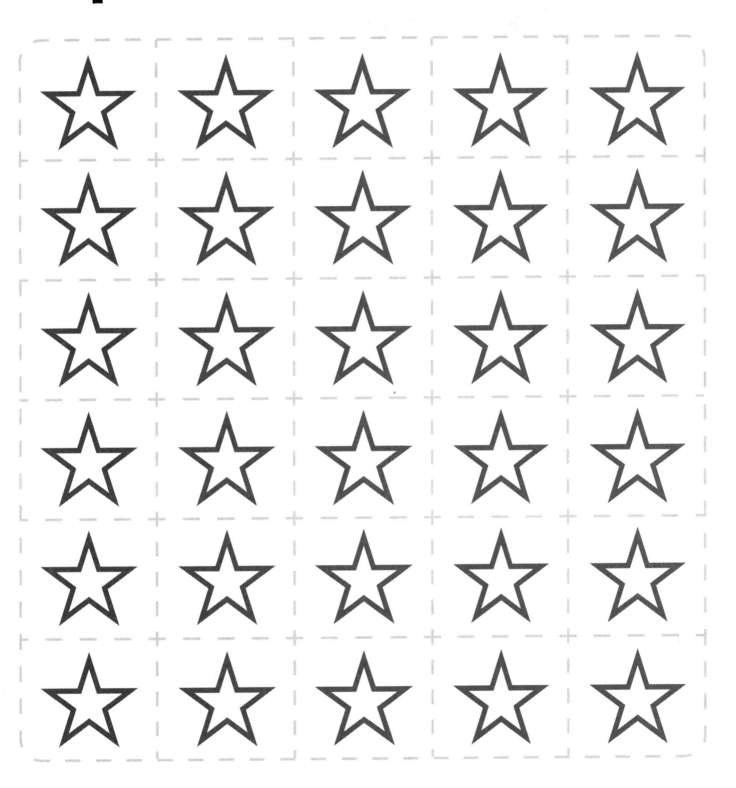

Phonics Word Lists for Other Blends

BEGINNING CLUSTERS

CR
crab
cradle
crane
crash
crayon
crib
cricket
crop
cross
crown
crumb
cry

DR
drab
dragon
drain
draw
dream
dress
drew
drill
drink
drop
drum
dry

FR
frame
frank
freckles
free
freeze
fresh
Friday
friend
frog
frozen
fruit
fry

BL
blab
black
blanket
bleach
blend
blink
blizzard
blob
bloom
blouse
blue
blush

GL

glad
glance
glass
glee
glide
glitch
glob
globe
gloom
gloss
glove
glow
glue

PL

place
plaid
plain
plan
plane
planet

plant
play
please
plenty
plug
plum

TW

tweed
tweet
tweezers
twelve
twice
twig
twin
twine
twinkle
twirl
twist
twister

QU

quack
quart
quarter
queen
quest
question
quick
quiet
quilt
quirk
quiz
quote

SC

scale
scalp
scamp
scan
scar
scare
scoop

scooter
scope
score
scout
scuba

SK

skate
sketch
ski
skid
skill
skin
skip
skirt
skit
skull
skink
sky

SM

smack

small
smart
smash
smear
smell
smile
smock
smog
smoke
smooth
smudge

SN

snack
snail
snake
snap
sneak
sneeze
sniff
snip
snoop

snore
snow
snuggle

SCR

scram
scramble
scrap
scrape
scratch
scrawl
scream
screech
screw
scribble
script
scrub

SQU

square
squash
squat

squeak
squeal
squeeze
squid
squint
squirm
squirrel
squirt
squish

STR
straight
strand
strange
straw
stray
streak
street
strength
string
stripe
strong
struggle

SPR
sprain
sprang
sprawl
spray
spread
sprig
spring
sprinkle
sprinkler
sprint
sprout
spruce

ENDING CLUSTERS

FT
craft
draft
drift
gift
left

lift
loft
raft
rift
shift
soft
tuft

LD
bald
bold
build
child
cold
gold
held
hold
mild
old
sold
wild

LT
belt
bolt
built
colt
fault
guilt
halt
jolt
melt
quilt
salt
tilt

MP
blimp
bump
camp
chimp
grump
jump
ramp

shrimp
stamp
swamp
thump
trump

ND
and
bend
end
find
hand
hound
land
mind
pound
sand
wand
wind

NK
bank

bunk
drink
honk
pink
plank
rink
sank
skunk
tank
think
trunk

NT
ant
bent
cent
front
hint
mint
paint
plant
rent

scent
sent
tent
want

RD
bird
board
cord
guard
hard
heard
herd
lard
sword
toward
word
yard

RK
ark
bark

clerk
fork
hark
jerk
lark
mark
park
perk
stork
work

ST
best
blast
chest
cost
dust
east
ghost
post
rest
test

west
wrist

Notes